ESPN
GUIDE TO
PSYCHO FAN
BEHAVIOR

D1456922

ESPN
BOOKS

GUI

PSYCH

BEHAV

DE TO

O FAN

IOR

EDITED BY **Warren St. John**

With Amir Blumenfeld, Spencer Hall, and Ethan Trex

WARNING
AND DISCLAIMER
(ESPECIALLY FOR STUPID PEOPLE)

This is not a book of advice, but rather a book of "advice." "Advice"—note the quotation marks—is actually the opposite of advice. When someone "advises" you to do something, you shouldn't actually do it. Instead you should marvel at the notion that someone would even contemplate doing something so stupid.

An example of advice would be: Choose a low interest rate credit card. An example of "advice" would be: Hold the end of a live extension cord in your teeth and jump in the bathtub. Paying low interest rates on your credit cards is smart. Jumping in the bath with a live electrical cord in your teeth is possibly the stupidest thing you could ever do to yourself. Remember that.

You alone are responsible for your actions and their consequences. If this book "advises" you to, say, cut off your own legs to avoid paying a bookie, or to coat your body in epoxy-based road striping paint before a big game, do not do these things. If you do, people will not only think you're an idiot, but they will also question your grasp of irony and sense of humor, which is far more humiliating.

Are we clear? Good.

Sincerely,
The Editors

CONTENTS

I

Introduction 12

Getting Started 16

At The Game 38

Fan Pride 74

Gambling and Fantasy Sports 88

Love, Work, and Other Hindrances

6

Between Games

7

Advanced Techniques

The Psycho Fan Hall of Fame

INTRODUCTION

THERE WAS A TIME when I considered myself a hard-core football fan. I had a picture of the late Alabama coach Bear Bryant on my office wall. I watched every televised game the Crimson Tide played, and occasionally flew cross-country to see them in person. I once listened to a game on the phone because I couldn't get it on television or the radio.

But several years ago, I decided to spend a few months on the road with the Tide's true **DIEHARDS** to figure out what being a fan was all about. The result was a book called *Rammer Jammer Yellow Hammer: A Road Trip Into the Heart of Fan Mania*. Like a lot of people, I highly recommend it.

The first thing I learned was that by the standard of **HARD-CORE** RVers, I was a bush leaguer. I started out by meeting a couple who'd skipped their daughter's wedding to go to an Alabama-Tennessee game. (They made the reception.) I met a guy who'd taken his name off a heart-transplant list to go to games. (Sadly but perhaps not surprisingly, he died.) I met folks who'd lost jobs and spouses because of their **ADDICTION** to sports. I went to an event for fans who'd named their kids after Bear Bryant—and six hundred people showed up.

I found out that there was no outdoing the truly devoted. I told a Florida Gators fanatic about the couple who'd skipped the wedding. He told me about a friend who'd crashed his Cessna into some trees on the way to a Gators-Mississippi State game, crawled out of the wreckage, thumbed a ride to the stadium, and made kickoff. Tell a hard-core fan you went to Woodstock, and he'll tell you he tuned Hendrix's guitar.

Over time, I began to see that being a hard-core fan wasn't just a freak of genetics. Being hard-core was—or at least could be—learned **BEHAVIOR**. You didn't skip your daughter's wedding for a game on a whim. That required forethought and a fully developed set of priorities (i.e., 1. my team. 2. everything else). You had to know what you were doing. You needed knowledge.

The implications of this discovery were huge. Everyone knows that, historically, teams with hard-core fans perform better. Well, what if you could learn to be more hard-core? You might actually help your team win more games. And what could be more hard-core than that?

So I quickly enlisted an expert team of sports psychopaths to show me—and, by extension, you—the finer points of **EXTREME** allegiance. Some of their advice will surprise you. Some may get you arrested or institutionalized, in which case a lawyer has emphatically instructed me to inform you: You're on your own. The point is, use this guide wisely.

If you aspire to be a truly **PSYCHO** fan, I think it will help you. At the very least, I hope you enjoy it, and that it brings your team glory on the field—unless, of course, your team is playing my team. In that case, bring a diaper. You're about to face the scariest fans in the universe.

See you in the stands,

WARREN ST. JOHN

Not recommended with children present

**May cause significant other to dump
you like a hot potato**

High risk of bodily harm

ICON KEY

Jail time likely

May result in institutionalization

Better reconsider

Just do it!!! Why not?!

Chapter One

Getting Started

Sports Around

STAYIN' WARM

SLED DOG RACIN'

SEAL CLUBBIN'

HOCKEY

GOLF
CRICKET
RUGBY
SOCCER

CURLING

HACKY SACKIN'

RODEO **GOLF**

BASKETBALL

JUST CHILLIN'

FOOTBALL

BASEBALL

NASCAR, WOO!

BULL-FIGHTIN'

BASEBALL

SOCCER

The World

MAKIN' STYLISH, AFFORDABLE FURNITURE

STAYIN' WARM

STAYIN' WARM

???-IN'

FIGURE SKATIN'

WRESTLIN'

SOCCER

TENNIS
SMOKIN'
POWER-LIFTIN'

MAKE DISCO DANCIN'

PING-PONG

BASEBALL
GOLF
SOCCER

CRICKET

KUNG FU

DROUGHT DODGIN'

SOCCER

HIPPO TAUNTIN'

RUNNIN' FOREVER

COUP-IN'

KICK-BOXIN'

CRICKET RUGBY

DROUGHT DODGIN'

GOLF CRICKET RUGBY

SHEEP TOSSIN' RUGBY

Fandom Throughout History: A Timeline

City of Troy adopts large wooden horse as soccer mascot and suffers horrible fate.

您不好

In Xian, China, the earliest recorded instance of fan hate mail, addressed to a player of the ancient Chinese football game cuju. The text is simple and to the point: **You. Not. Good.**

1300 BC	1000 BC	800 BC	776 BC

Bookies across the Levant absorb huge losses when Goliath of Gath falls to David of the Israelites. "All credit to the Big Guy," says David, perplexingly, in victory.

Coroebus, the first-ever Olympic track-and-field champion, celebrates his victory in the 192-meter stade race by leaping, all naked and sweaty, into the crowd. The towel and running shorts are invented immediately thereafter.

Romans debut swimsuit issue in *Agonis Picturis* ("Sports Pictured"). Full pictorial available in mosaic to subscribers only.

Vikings, in their horned helmets, fur boots, and purple-and-gold jerseys, attack England, bringing the concept of team uniforms to the British Isles.

212 BC   **455 AD**   **976 AD**   **1206-1294 AD**

Soccer hooligans sack Rome.

First sports dynasty ever emerges in central Mongolia as the unstoppable Mongol Horde flourishes under general manager Genghis Khan. A primitive version of "We Will Rock You" is debuted for use at pep rallies and before razing whole cities.

Magellan witnesses first recorded use of the foam finger—crafted from harvested sea sponges—during heated cockfight in the Philippines. Donning the porous pointer, the Portuguese boatman is stoned when he unknowingly makes a crass gesture to the crowd. (Thus, "flipping the bird.")

American Revolution is sparked when fans petition for management changes at the "New Englande Football Teaem of Bostonne."

1521 AD   **1633 AD**   **1776 AD**   **1848 AD**

Spanish Inquisition forces Galileo to recant heliocentrism and his firm belief that "defense wins championships."

Instant replay fails to decide outcome of Crimean War.

Streaker interrupts Battle of Verdun, prolonging what was already the lengthiest confrontation in World War I history.

NBA's new arena fireworks—particularly the gas torches outside the entry tunnels—create massive fuel shortages in the United States.

1916 AD   **1948-49 AD**   **1973 AD**   **1991 AD**

Fans thrill as civil war-torn China decides its fate with an epic table tennis match between Mao Zedong, ping-pong master of the Reds, and Chiang Kai-shek, American puppet. The Communist overlord wins a tiebreaker, 21-20, to wrest control of the mainland. Zedong (then known by his maiden name, Tse-tung) credits fans' innovative "wave" cheer with boosting his spirits during the contest.

Bud Bowl III ends in a forfeit as Bud Light fans clash with Bud fans, injuring 16 and ending the life of Bud Dry, who was shattered during the rioting.

Depressed by grunge music and repeated watchings of *Reality Bites*, baseball breaks up with its fan base to "just go out West and find myself, man." Fan base copes by moving into a rent-controlled New York City apartment with five wacky, telegenic friends, all of whom promise to be there "when the rain starts to fall."

Longtime practice of throwing bowl game symbols—roses, oranges, sugar, et al—onto the field backfires as college football fans litter the turf with hundreds of kittens at the 2000 ASPCA Spay-or-Neuter-Your-Cat Bowl.

1994 AD   **1995 AD**   **2000 AD**   **2004 AD**

Tired of wearing flannel, baseball reconciles with fan base, but only after hitting the gym really, really hard.

In a similarly chilling scene, 34 fans, players, and sideline personnel at the Starbucks Bowl in Seattle are injured by venti cups of scalding hot coffee thrown by fans of the winning South Carolina Tech Firehogs.

Fan Gear Essentials for a New Age

Three items that every true fan must own are a beer helmet, a team jersey, and a pair of team-colored pants otherwise known as Zubaz. (Jeans are for datin', Zubaz are for passion.) Important note: The beer helmet serves as cruise control, not driving. Holding a beer in one's hand at all times is obviously still required.

Ⓐ Foam Finger Think your team's No. 1? Prove it.*
Can also be replaced at your discretion with a bit of mojo: a rally monkey made of socks, a rubber chicken, a catheter, the opposing team's mascot with a noose around its neck. Whatever you choose, make sure you can shake it with ease at a TV camera while acting preposterously excited.

....

Ⓑ Road Flare Especially handy at Italian soccer matches, it lets opposing fans know that their team has broken down and they had better call AAA.

....

Ⓒ Cell Phone Useful for in-game gloating, score-checking, postgame pizza ordering, and, when truly unavoidable, calling significant others.

....

Ⓓ Lucky Underwear Worn During 1993 Playoffs What started out as a pair of loose boxer briefs now resembles a pair of jockeys clinging to their last atoms of structural integrity. What your spouse calls "biohazard-level funk" you call "years of positive karma."

....

Ⓔ ThunderStix Great for playing "Wipeout" and other stadium classics on the back of the seat in front of you. Or, in the case of backless bleachers, for making friends by playing drums on some poor sap's shoulder blades.

....

Ⓕ Beer Belly Not only economical, but also an excuse for that rapidly advancing waistline, the Beer Belly grants you pioneer-style independence while you skirt those pesky rules against bringing alcohol into the stadium. Better still, consumption of contents creates the illusion that spectating helps you shed weight.

....

Ⓖ Knee Brace In case injury strikes and the coach signals for you to take the field for your beleaguered team.

....

Ⓗ Bottle of Chloroform Useful for sedating the overly vocal rival sitting next to you, as well as for knocking yourself out in the event of a catastrophic loss.

Replica Jerseys: Some Rules Apply

Sure, you can say you have a favorite player, but proof is when you've shelled out a hundred bucks for your stud's shiny jersey. Work out enough, and people might start mistaking you for LeBron, even though you're 5'10" and white. You can, however, go too far. A great garment for all manner of settings, the replica jersey is ill-suited for others. Here's a handy guide:

Situation	Touchdown	Fumble
BOWL GAME	👍	
JOB INTERVIEW		👎
SPORTS CARD SHOW	👍	
FUNERAL (YOUR MOTHER'S)		👎
FUNERAL (ACQUAINTANCE'S)	👍 BUT ONLY IF AUTHENTIC	
WATCHING THE GAME WITH BUDS	👍	
PAROLE HEARING		👎
PICK-UP GAME (IF YOU'RE GOOD)	👍	
PICK-UP GAME (IF YOU SUCK)		👎
IMPERSONATING PLAYER TO PICK UP LADIES	👍 BUT POTENTIALLY A FELONY	

Buying a TV

If you're going to watch the game at home, you'll need a screen that does the action justice. How much should you spend? Piece of cake. Take your bank account balance and add the pawn value of your spouse's wedding ring. Now run out and buy the biggest TV you can find before she gets wind of your plans.

Game Over: When It's Safe to Turn Off a Basketball Game

"Come on, Honey. They're down 39 and there's only two minutes left, I think we can turn the TV off now and have dinner. I made your favorite."

That all sounds reasonable ... if you're married to a Nazi prison guard.

A true fan knows that a steal and a three-pointer takes four seconds, max. Mathematically speaking, the game is never "over" until the scoring margin is greater than the number of seconds on the clock divided by four and multiplied by three.

> **(SECONDS LEFT / 4) X 3 =**
> **MAXIMUM DEFICIT THAT CAN BE OVERCOME**

Thus, in the example above, the correct response would be, "As long as we're within 90, anything can happen. And you can forget about dinner. You know my policy: I only eat when we win."

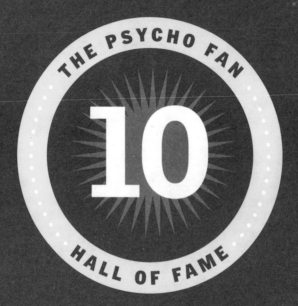

Beverly Grant

A superior court judge in Tacoma, Washington, Grant opened a first-degree manslaughter sentencing in the death of a local man by urging everyone in her courtroom to yell, "Go Seahawks!," two days before the team faced the Steelers in Super Bowl XL. When the response was tepid, she demanded that onlookers shout it out again. The prosecutor later took umbrage: "One family is seeing a son go off to prison, and one family is here to find justice for a murdered loved one. Do you think they want to root for the Seahawks?"

After the Steelers defeated the Seahawks, 21-10, the judge issued a warrant for the Seahawks defense. The charge: failure to appear.

Learn to

Harness Your

Has your team gone
on an 11-0 run since you flipped
your hat backwards? Does it only
win important games when you watch
them at a certain friend's house?
These aren't coincidences. They're
scientifically proven causalities, and
when you learn how to identify
and control them, you can all but
guarantee success!

Praying: A How-To

Praying is no myth. It can make any desired outcome in sports a reality. (Why else would so many fans rely on it?) But keep in mind that it can also backfire if done incorrectly.

Always use proper form Intertwine your fingers, raise your hands to a level just below your nose, and close your eyes. If possible, drop to your knees.

Pray like you mean it "Please God, if you help me out just this once, I promise to stop stealing toner cartridges from work" is much more plausible than "I promise to be an attentive and loving husband."

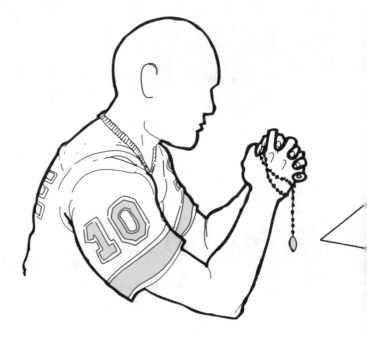

Don't overdo it If you're praying effectively, you should see results quickly. But prayer is like bluffing in poker—use it too often, and its value diminishes. Never, for example, pray in the first half of a game. Better yet, wait for the postseason, unless your magic number is one with none to play. And pray only once per playoff series per team per sport. That's right. No praying for a break in Game 6 and Game 7.

And, finally, every once in a while, it's okay to pray for a miracle. (How else do you think Frank Reich became a household name?)

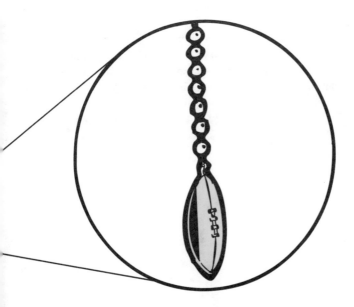

The Painful Truth About Your Sports Tattoo

As we all know, tattoos aren't just for the currently incarcerated and for drunk girls on spring break; they're also the ultimate sign of sports loyalty. But don't forget that they're permanent and initially quite painful. So before you run out to get a tat, give it at least five or 10 minutes of thought.

→ It's always better to get a tattoo honoring a team than a tattoo honoring a player. The team will always be around,* but in a few months or years that "Grant Hill—Indestructible" or "In Romo We Trust" might look a little silly.

→ A logo alone looks a little sparse. How about sprucing things up with RULES!! underneath it? Wow, that looks so much better.

→ If your favorite team has a country-western flair, like the Texas Longhorns or the Dallas Cowboys, you may want to consider branding instead. With a coat hanger and open flame, this is a do-it-yourself proposition. Cows do it all the time.

Exceptions: Franchises in Cleveland, Los Angeles, and any city in Canada.

Postgame Cooldown Period

When it comes to scheduling conflicts, most sports fans know the math: You take the estimated start time, and allot yourself at least three hours of uninterrupted TV viewing. That means no 8 p.m. dinner if the game starts at 6, no 5 p.m. wedding if the game starts at 4, and no 2 p.m. "kid's first piano recital" if the game starts at noon.

However, most fans get themselves into trouble when they try to apply this formula to big games. The "win-or-go-home" games. The bowl games. The Game 7 games. While these contests generally last around three hours, you do not under any circumstance want to make plans for at least six hours after start time (and preferably eight). Here's why: Though the game may end on time, you may not be emotionally prepared for the event you promised to attend, regardless of who wins.

Yes, it may seem rude to skip your daughter's wedding, even though she specifically planned it for two hours after the game ended. However, when the priest asks if anybody has any reason why these two should not be married, and you shout "a porous defense and inexperienced quarterback play!," that's even ruder.

Skipping a funeral is likewise considered poor social etiquette, but so is fist-pumping your way through the eulogy because you're still on cloud nine after that incredible buzzer beater.

So take the high road. While your loved ones may be absolutely livid that you seemingly skipped important family gatherings for no reason at all, you'll know that you saved yourself from saying or doing something truly horrific.

Chapter Two

At the Game

Getting There

As everyone knows, truly hard-core fans live in drainage culverts underneath stadiums. But if you're one of those fair-weather types who must travel to the big game, you have a range of options.

Hitchhiking

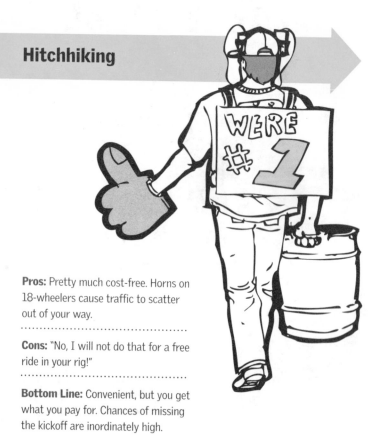

Pros: Pretty much cost-free. Horns on 18-wheelers cause traffic to scatter out of your way.

Cons: "No, I will not do that for a free ride in your rig!"

Bottom Line: Convenient, but you get what you pay for. Chances of missing the kickoff are inordinately high.

Driving Your Own Car

Pros: Leave when you want to. Ideal for low-level tailgating.

....

Cons: Traffic, parking, risk of damage to your car if attacked by rival fans, DUI.

....

Bottom Line: A good option for John Q. Average Sports Fan, but leave home early.

RVing

Pros: Bathroom, fridge included. Tells others: I freaking, LOVE this team.

Cons: Parking, traffic, $100K price tag, horrible gas mileage. Note: Whatever you do in that bathroom is stored in onboard tank. (Just sayin'.)

Bottom Line: Any and all impracticality outweighed by the intimidating message it sends to other fans: We love our team so much, we drove our house to the stadium.

Pros: Traffic, parking—no problem! Awesome view of the field.

Cons: Expensive, hell on windy days.

Bottom Line: Next to living in a culvert beneath the stadium, this is as hard-core as it gets. Go for it!

Commandeering a Blimp

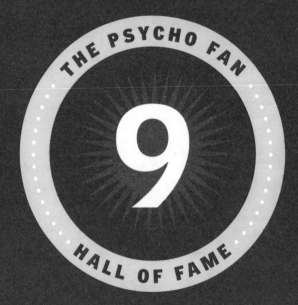

Glenn Timmerman

The self-proclaimed No. 1 fan of the Chicago Bears, Timmerman has 55 autographs of current and former players tattooed on his body. As soon as he gets a signature, he runs right over to his favorite tat parlor to have it etched into his flesh. His first: Otis Ryan. No. 55: Mike Singletary.

He dreads the day when a memorabilia collector makes him an offer he can't refuse for that Hunter Hillenmeyer on his right delt.

Clothes and the Weather:
An Inverse Relationship

As humans, we're taught at an early age that the colder it is outside, the more clothing you must wear. Not to call your mother a filthy liar, but in football, the opposite is true.

Because the season begins in August and ends in January, weather conditions run the gamut. Late-summer games in Arizona might be 150° warmer than those played in Chicago in midwinter. How do you parlay those variations into team spirit? By shedding or donning clothing.

The key to demonstrating your undying support is to show the players that no matter how tough things get on the field, you're the one who's truly suffering. Fans from warm-weather cities should, for example, prove their mettle by bundling up. If you think it's hard-core to sit through a sub-zero temperature game in your boxers, try going to a 103° Cardinals game in a parka. Those nude, freezing Bears fans in December are just getting chilly; you're the one risking dehydration, nausea, and heat stroke. Feeling particularly devoted? Limit your water intake to a couple of ounces per quarter. Doctors clearly advise against this, but you don't see any of them crying after a loss. (For the record, we don't recommend crying. The liquid in your tear ducts might be the only thing keeping you alive.)

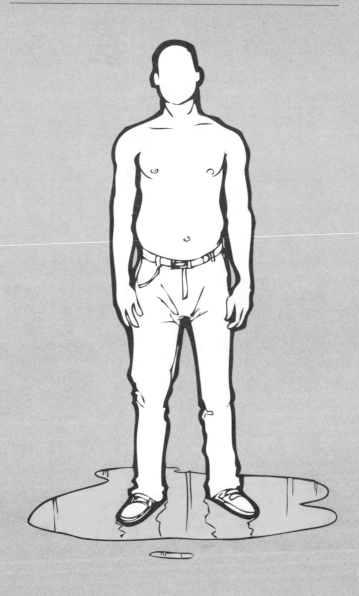

A User's Guide to Body Paint

Many people think that painting your body for a sporting event is a simple affair. Step 1: Paint body. Step 2: Go to game and jump around like an idiot. While they're definitely right about Step 2, they're shortchanging the technical acumen required to produce the desired effect.

The most important step in the body-painting process is not the painting of the body, but, rather, choosing what type of paint to use. Your selection says everything about what kind of fan you are.

Water-Based Paint

Pros: Washes off easily.

Cons: Runs in a rainstorm.

Bottom Line: If you're going to the trouble of painting yourself to let everyone know how devoted you are, why would you slather yourself in something that will run from a single bead of sweat? Water-based paints are for fair-weather fans and wimps.

Oil-Based House Paints

Pros: Cheap. Durable. Can be applied with a roller or paint gun.

Cons: Requires a turpentine shower and lots of rags to remove.

Additional Con: Can produce intoxicating fumes.
Additional Pro: Can produce intoxicating fumes.

Observation: Rain-, cocktail-, and sweat-proof, this is the preferred method for hard-core fans whose team colors don't run.

Bottom Line: Now we're talking.

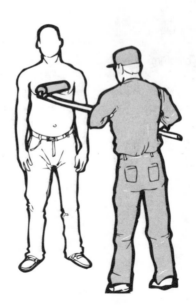

Pros: Not. Coming. Off.

....

Cons: If applied haphazardly, it can harden into an indestructible shell. May require Jaws of Life rescue. Expensive.

....

Observation: No one will ever accuse you of being a fair-weather fan if you lather your body with this stuff. Rainproof, fireproof, jackhammer-proof—you name it—this stuff lasts.

....

Bottom Line: The ultimate Psycho Fan statement.

 Forever Brand™ Epoxy-Based Road-Striping Paint

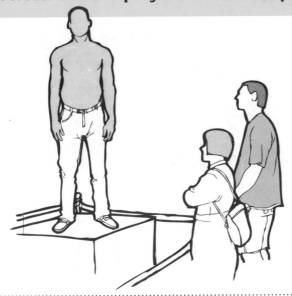

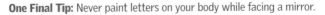

One Final Tip: Never paint letters on your body while facing a mirror.

....

How to Translate Scalper Lingo

When buying tickets from a scalper, it's important to note that you're usually not dealing with the most honest person on the planet. This handy chart will help you decipher where your seats are likely to be.

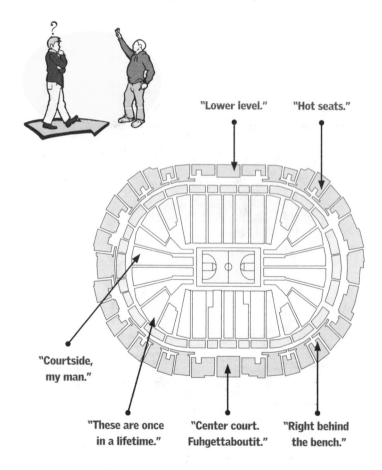

"Lower level."   "Hot seats."

"Courtside,
my man."

"These are once
in a lifetime."   "Center court.
Fuhgettaboutit."   "Right behind
the bench."

Scoring Student Tickets
(Or, Geeks Don't Want No Seats)

Nothing's worse than not having a ticket to the big game, especially when you don't have the disposable income, mirrored sunglasses, and easily concealed knife required for a transaction with a scalper. For pro sports, this means you're out of luck unless you sneak through the gate disguised as a peanut vendor.

College sports offer a glimmer of hope, though, because most schools reserve a section of seats at a steeply discounted price for students. The imperative for any real fan is clear: Get into those seats at any cost. But how? Find a nerd.

Every college has nerds, and odds are they won't be using their tickets on gameday. They'll be doing nerdy things instead. Don't ask us what they are; we're not nerds. To find a nerd, roam the campus—in front of the library is a good place to start—and ask aloud for directions to the local nerditorium. When someone replies that nerditorium isn't a real word, stop right there. You've found your mark. Start the negotiation at $5 below face value.

How a True Sports Purist Fills
Out an All-Star Ballot

Grab a handful of ballots. Check off the starter from your favorite team at every position. Repeat as often as possible before exiting the stadium. If the event in question is the Pro Bowl, don't bother voting. You're better than that.

Sneaking Down: Tapping the Human Vulture in You

There's no greater thrill, no more inspiring sign of devotion than starving yourself to save $200 for lower-level seats ... "Yeah, I lost 35 pounds this week, but I've never felt better! Stop worrying about me, Mom! No, *you* have your priorities out of whack!"

That works, but for those who like eating too much to give it up, there's a healthier, time-tested method for watching your favorite team up close and personal: sneaking down. And unlike its seedy cousin sneaking in, sneaking down does not require an inside job.

Step 1: Buy the worst seat available. The nosebleed section of a basketball arena serves two purposes. First, your purloined seats will seem so much better after you spend the first half perched above the JumboTron. Second and more important, the crow's-nest height will give you a clear view of the finest seats in the house.

Step 2: Don't bother watching the action. This shouldn't be too difficult since you'll have a hard time determining if that last shot was a two, a three, or the team mascot doing a flip-dunk off the trampoline during a timeout. Instead scope out the empty seats. Don't get too greedy—nothing courtside, for example. Anything above the tenth row is fair game and close enough to the hardwood for you to smell the players (if that's your thing).

Step 3: To make certain you'll find those seats once you're down on the floor, assign them human markers, e.g., "Four next to the cowboy and the cheesehead!" The view from on high looks much different than the view from below.

Step 4: Make your move at halftime when there's a heavy flow of traffic. Have a line ready for the usher just in case. "Uh, I thought this was section 500, row 44. My bad!"

Stadium Signage: Your Ticket to TV Glory

Of the thousands of signs brought into every major sporting event in this country, only a choice few get the glory of two or three seconds on live TV. But with a little know-how, you can increase your odds of joining the elite tier of society known as Those Who Have Been Televised.

METHOD 1: THE TRIED AND THE TRUE

The surest way to get on TV is to suck up to the network people broadcasting the game. The problem is, lots of other people will be using this same strategy, so you have to suck up much more aggressively than the obsequious suck-ups around you. The network's call letters are all-important, of course, but if you can also figure out a way to incorporate one of the commentators' names in your sign, well, make room for an Emmy on your trophy shelf because you're going to be on ... the ... air.

Step 1: Grab some Magic Markers and a poster board.

Step 2: Identify which network is broadcasting your game.

Step 3: Write the network's call letters in a vertical line on a napkin or a piece of notebook paper. For example:

Step 4: While there are many perfectly legitimate things for a fan to say about a broadcaster, most are not nearly flattering enough to get you on TV. So think of something really flattering. Flattering enough to make you blush—say, "When I think of Bob Costas, I get a tingly feeling all over." Good! Now render that general idea using the letters N, B, and C, and you're on your way to TV stardom. How about ...

The Fox Challenge

The media conglomerate spell-out works just fine for networks whose call letters are your basic consonants and vowels. But what do you do with the x in Fox? That's a real brainteaser. But believe it or not, there are non-scientific words and proper names that begin with the letter x. Here are a few to get you started: Xylophone, X-ray, Xtra, and Xerxes.

Again, flatter:

METHOD 2: PATHETIC SIGNS

Another surefire way to get on television is to make a sign lamenting how much your team sucks. Pathetic works on TV; it makes the home audience feel superior. Network executives know this. Good pathetic signs include the following:

Note: Despite its former effectiveness, we do not recommend putting a grocery bag over your head. While the paper bag will almost certainly get you on TV, people will confuse you with the Unknown Comic. (And if you use a plastic bag, the Suffocated Comic.)

Boos and Booze: The Corollary

Pleasure of Sporting Event

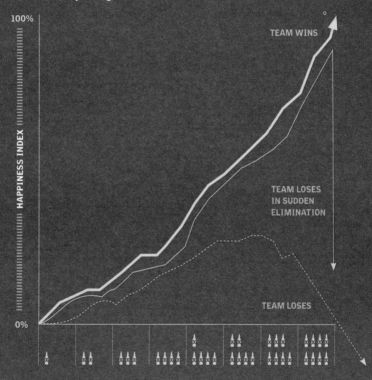

Alcohol Consumption
(Measured in trips to concession stand)

The T-Shirt Cannon and You

How many times have you been sitting at a game and said to yourself, Man, this is fun, but an XXXL Hanes Beefy T would make it better? If you're like the rest of us, it's almost every time you go to the arena. Thankfully, the T-shirt cannon has caught on in recent years. After its invention by weapons engineers from a country with a well-dressed but nonthreatening military (hint: Italy), the T-shirt cannon has become a staple at American sporting events. As a fan, there is no sweeter in-game plum to be picked than catching a $3.99 article of clothing fired at you by the team mascot (disturbingly, often someone who misses high school ROTC). Here's how to grab one:

Take off the shirt you're wearing It may not be a pretty sight, but you're exponentially more likely to draw the shooter's eye if your massive gut is in obvious need of covering.

Be enthusiastic Jump up and down. Scream. Wave your arms. Hoist a sign with a target painted on it.

Limber up The overwhelming majority of ballpark swagmeisters are not ex-Marine Corps snipers, so they lack aim. Get ready to dive, grapple, and claw your way to the bounty if that's what it takes to land a T with the thread count of a dollar-store pillowcase.

Wear it proudly When you finally score your swell, 50/50 cotton-poly blend of a trophy, don't doubt the gravity of the achievement. Sure, you don't really need a Sierra Mist billboard, but that's not important. What is important is that you outwitted, outran, and outboxed every other jerk in the arena to get it, and no one can take that away from you.

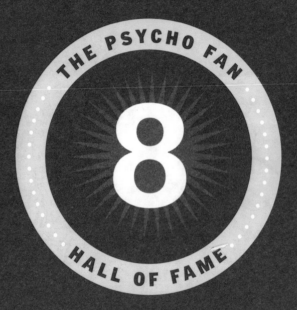

Colleen Pavelka

Nine months pregnant, Pavelka, 28, didn't want to force her husband to choose between going to a Bears-Saints playoff game and attending the birth of their child. So she persuaded her obstetrician to induce labor early, freeing up her husband on gameday.

The Bears won, 39-14, and advanced to the Super Bowl.
Mark Patrick Pavelka was born on Friday, January 19, 2007.
Safe bet that Colleen Pavelka hasn't had to do the dishes since.

All's Fair in Catching Foul Balls

Most sporting events showcase the greatness of others: someone drilling an amazing three or throwing an unbelievable pass. Baseball, however, offers a unique opportunity to demonstrate your own athletic prowess every time a home run or a foul ball reaches the stands. The moment that lustrous orb enters Fanland, you're under only one directive: Catch it at any cost.

> Keep your eye on the ball. Unlike the hectoring advice yelled at you by your abusive uncle at Little League games, this maxim is crucially important in ball grabbing. (But don't call it ball grabbing.)

As soon as you determine that the majestic object of your deepest desire is going to land in your section, assess where it's going to drop and do whatever it takes to get there. Don't be shy about throwing elbows at the people standing between you and ground zero; they'd be doing the same thing to you if they were standing in you shoes. Under no circumstances should you hesitate if the ball looks to be coming down a few rows in front of you. Lunge. If that old woman was really worried about getting crushed by a flying fan, she'd have gone to a bridge game instead.

> If the ball is destined to become a historic piece of memorabilia that Todd McFarlane will pay millions to purchase, things get trickier. There will inevitably be large scrums and ensuing legal battles for such a ball. Think ahead by bringing your lawyer to the game.

> To keep or not to keep, that's the question. Catch a home run ball hit by a player from a particularly nasty rival (think Cubs-Cardinals or Yanks-Sox), and fellow fans will urge you to dump it back on the field. It's childish, yes, but best to do what they say. Ten thousand drunken Yankee fans can be wrong, but they won't know it until after they've beaten you to a pulp.

➡ Once you've secured the ball, hold it aloft for a round of applause. This will rank as one of the most memorable moments of your life, right up there with losing your virginity and attending your second parole hearing, so savor it. Hold up a single index finger, because you really are No. 1, Champ.

➡ At this point, you will be faced with the toughest decision in a ball catcher's life: Do you buckle to the simpering kid at your feet? Mysteriously, catching a foul ball or a homer makes five or six hollow-eyed and malnourished 8-year-olds materialize in your midst. They want your souvenir. Ignore them.

➡ Display the ball proudly. Throw it right up on the mantle, even if it means knocking aside some crummy pottery your kid cooked up at camp. Nobody's going to be impressed by that, but when they see that you've got a foul ball Otis Nixon hit in 1996, they're sure to let out an amazed, "Huh?" Well done.

Free Throw Distractions: Your Team Needs You

We've all been there before. You're at the game when the opposing team's best player steps to the free throw line, down by one with only a few seconds left. Lucky for you, your seat is directly in his line of vision. He can't eyeball the rim without fixing you in his corneas. It's your time to shine. You bang those ThunderStix into a cacophonous blur. His first attempt goes in. On his second, you couple your Thunderstixing with unabashedly horrific screams. Swish! Deep down, you know that you alone are responsible for the loss.

What could you have done differently? Use your Thunderstix more creatively. Instead of banging them together in a futile bid at ear-shattering and eye-fogging distraction, persuade your arena mates to move them in a slow, swirling pattern. The calm, gentle motions, when performed to choreographed perfection, will make it appear as if the basket is moving. This optical illusion causes mild vertigo in most adult males, and you will find nothing that makes you prouder than making the opposing free throw shooter hurl on his Jordans before he tosses up a brick.

Consider alternative techniques If you lack the charisma to persuade an entire quarter of the arena to move in unison with you, don't despair. There are independent measures you can take. Smuggle in a giant, collapsible, spiraling hypnosis disc. Nothing too ostentatious; a 15-foot radius will do. As the shooter steps to the line, begin rotation. Scientific fan fact: Sinking free throws when deep in REM sleep is nearly impossible. Another option: Bring a fold-up, cardboard cutout of the opposing player's wife to the game, and when he toes the line, start talking trash, loudly and profanely to the cutout until he rushes to her aid. You might get punched in the face by a man twice your size, but not before he's whistled for a blatant lane violation.

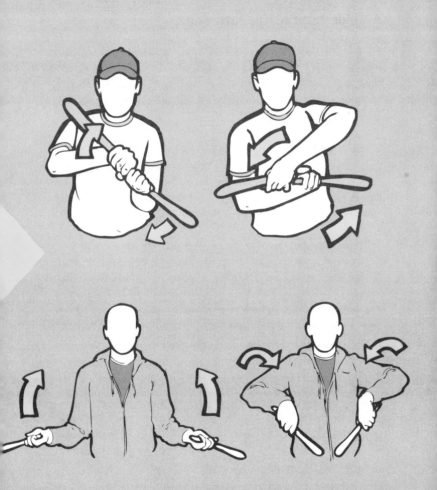

A Guide to Stadium Bathrooms

You knew this would happen when you drank seven beers before you got
through the gate, but now you've got to go—*really bad*. But you came to
watch the game, not the backs of the jerks ahead of you in the long line
to the filthy men's room. How do you get maximum relief with minimum
impact on the game clock?

Bottle It Up Discretely slip a soda bottle, a personal urinal, or another
container into your pants, and take care of business. Just don't feel hurt
when your friends refuse to high-five you for the rest of the game. Adult
diapers have also reached a level of comfort and absorbency that your
incontinent grandparents could only have dreamed about.

In Through the Out Door Not just a great Zeppelin record; also a fantastic
tactic for cutting the line. Slip in through the exit while freshly relieved sports
fans are filing out, scamper up to a free urinal, and let the good times flow.

The Boy Who Cried Puke Bum-rush the line while hollering, "Lemme
through! I'm gonna barf!" Crash through the door of a stall, and take care
of your business. If anyone asks you why you didn't vomit, say, "What?
Were you hoping I'd be sick? Jerk."

 All the World's a Urinal Pee in any corner of the stadium. So long as you
don't get arrested for public urination, you won't miss a play!

Noise-o-Meters: Pure Science

You might think that animated noise-o-meter doesn't truly calibrate decibel
levels, but it does. When it goads you on by flashing the text "We can't hear
you!!!," it actually means you can't be heard. So you'd better start yelling
and make that animation explode before the timeout ends. Your team is
depending on it.

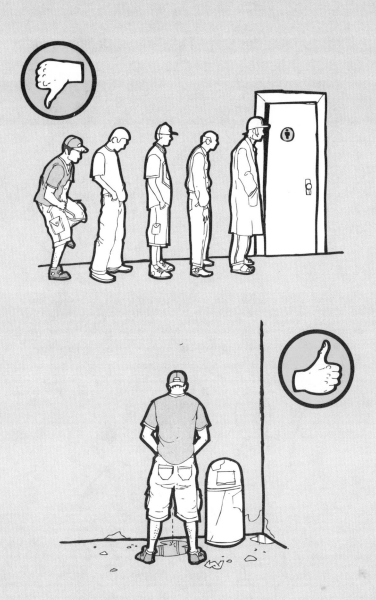

Of High-Fives, Hugs, and Fist-Bumps: Celebrating

Nothing beats going to a game, particularly if you're starved for human contact. Sure, nobody's going to want you touching them during the tailgate, and it's best to keep your hands to yourself through the "rockets' red glare" portion of the national anthem at least. Beyond that, though, there's no better place to rub skin than within the confines of a home-team crowd. Move slowly, but gradually ramp up.

The High-Five

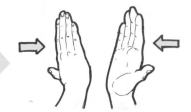

From 300-pound Teamsters to the cute brunette sitting next to you, everyone loves a good high-five after a big play. There's absolutely no excuse for not celebrating. You don't want to seem desperate, though, so reserve the two-handed double high-five for legitimately huge plays, like interceptions, breakaway dunks, and homers.

The Fan Hug

When even the double high-five doesn't properly express your excitement, you might need to resort to the fan hug. Special-teams touchdowns, furious comebacks, and virtually any Columbia University football victory are all legitimate reasons to turn to your neighbor, scream, "Wa-hooooo!," and throw open your arms. He or she will know you're going for a fan hug and reciprocate.

The Fan Kiss

No longer just for Italian soccer fans, the fan kiss can be deployed in moments of extreme excitement. Winning the Super Bowl or World Series, beating Duke at hoops, and staying awake long enough to witness the end of a quintuple-overtime playoff hockey game are all occasions when you can look deep into the eyes of the fan next to you and lay a smooch on him. (Or better still, her.) Remember: absolutely no tongue. This is a game, not the third round of Spin the Bottle.

Fighting a Mascot

From time to time, your life as a fan might involve mixing it up with a mascot. Whether your encounter involves a simple shoving match, advanced fisticuffs, or the melee tactics of an all-out riot, here are the techniques you'll need to master to survive the face-off.

> **Size up your enemy** Be aware that the eyes of a giant foam mascot do not usually correspond with the eyes of the person inside the costume. Consequently, eye-gouge maneuvers are almost totally useless. Conversely, bulky, vision-impairing headgear puts mascots at a disadvantage when attacked from behind. Surprise is your friend.

Do not allow the match to get to the ground It's a little-known fact that most mascots are superb grapplers. Part of their prowess comes from the adrenaline rush of being blindsided (see helmet limitations, above), but the greater advantage is the slippery plush of the mascot's outfit. While you're losing your grip on the Phillie Phanatic's slick, hairy hide, he's working you into an excruciating, figure-four leg lock—a nightmare scenario that careless fans too often fail to consider before they suffer the cruel laughter of a national TV audience.

Win and advance quickly Unless you're working in a riot situation, security will likely end your mascot fracas in less than a minute. But it's worth remembering that while you were pounding back nachos in the second deck, your opponent was shedding 10 pounds of water weight in that full-body moose suit. Avoid a long engagement by striking decisively and fleeing quickly. Consider dyeing your hair and growing a mustache while laying low after the incident.

Never pick a fight with a live animal mascot You are no match for an actual steer or buffalo, so don't even think about it.

Head: Limits peripheral vision, distorts balance. Weight can help you get in a really good piledriver.

Heart: With the stifling heat and water loss inside the suit, you can try to maneuver him into a heart attack.

Fur: If all else fails, synthetic fur is highly flammable.

Groin: Because baby mascots don't come from the stork.

3

Fan Pride

Strategies for Effective Heckling

If you can't get on the court yourself, you can always help the team win by mentally breaking down the opposition. Players will tell you they can't hear hecklers, but that's a lie. How do you think Spike Lee got so famous? A good heckler is at least as valuable to a team as a point guard who protects the ball. Some pointers to increase your efficiency:

⟹ Always start with, "Hey, [player's name]!" It's just proper etiquette.

⟹ Don't bother making a sign; most players aren't big readers. But if you absolutely must, make it an easily interpreted, Egyptian-style pictogram. We suggest [picture of the player] + [picture of a bird] + [picture of a pyramid].

⟹ Do your homework before you heckle. For instance, if you want to rank on a player's mama, try to confirm that she's still alive. It would be really mean-spirited to bring her up if she's not.

⟹ Lots of people think you can use the "Over-rated!" chant only when you've beaten a highly ranked opponent. Not true. The inventive fan will use it at any moment. Are you beating a winless team? Has anyone discussed them as being among the worst of all time? Then they're probably overrated. Take that, Duke football!

⟹ Players are pretty much immune to the tired old "You suck!" Try something utterly confusing instead. "Hey! Twenty-five! Banana stardust transmission!" When he stops to figure it out, a pass will hit him in the face. "Keep your eye on the ball, son!"

Last Resort
Players might be able to zone out vicious heckling, but not even the Dalai Lama himself can ignore being jabbed in the side.

How to be a College Sports Booster

Who says you need to run a sub-4.5 40 to be team MVP? If you've got a fat wallet and flexible morals, you don't even need to suit up. In the wildly competitive world of prep recruiting, a good booster makes all the difference.

Think you have what it takes? Try this quiz.

- Can you land a job for that speedy linebacker's recently-paroled brother/mother/cousin/neighbor? Something with a window, a company Lexus, and three weeks' paid vacation?

- Are you willing to reduce your entire wardrobe to two items: khaki slacks and a golf shirt with a team logo on the front?

- Do you find yourself launching into long, rambling monologues about how the NCAA's an unjust socialist regime and these kids should be paid a few hundred grand a year to cover the cost of living?

- Can you palm a hundred-dollar bill and shake it into a recruit's hand while telling him you'd "love to have him here" and "could make it worth his while?"

- Do you own a duffel bag that can be stuffed with cash and dropped behind a tree? At the park? At midnight? Can you come alone?

If you answered yes to any of these questions, congrats—you've made the team. See you in the V.I.P. Box!

The Art of Gloating

You might have had parents, probably liberal wacko types, who told you that gloating is wrong. They probably preached the importance of being a gracious winner and loser. That was all well and good for the 20th century, but today's world necessitates hard-core gloating after a win.

Take, for example, when your team beats your buddy's team. Make no mistake: It means you are a better person than he is. Whatever deity you worship loves you more. Yes, your pal makes more money and has a better-looking wife. Sure, he seems happier. But your team won, and because of that, he's dying inside. It's your job and responsibility, as a true friend and rabid sports fan, to really, really rub it in, even if it leaves him so despondent he wants to hurt himself. See "Listening to the Game at School Plays, Weddings, Funerals, and Other Nuisances," page 118.

Gloating Phone Call Dos and Don'ts

You're at home watching your team play its hated rival. Your buddy is across town on his sofa supporting that rival team. The tide turns in your favor thanks to a ferocious dunk, a special-teams touchdown, or a mammoth home run. Do you whip out your phone and call him? Not so fast, my friend. Making gloating phone calls is an art form, and you certainly don't want to breach the densely layered etiquette for such things.

- A halftime phone call is acceptable, but don't be too smug. Mention your squad's shortcomings and your rival's strengths. This will make you seem magnanimous, and you don't want to look like a jerk … yet. You'll look like a jerk plenty when you paint "State RULES!!!" on the hood of his car.

- Never, ever brag about the game before it's over. Even if your team is up 72-10 with a minute left to play, resist the urge to rub it in. The sports gods will find some sort of 64-point play with which to punish that kind of hubris. In fact, they'll relish the opportunity. Sports gods don't often get a chance to be creative.

- If your team is on the wrong end of a blowout, call to "concede" with five minutes left on the clock. Your buddy will mistake this for maturity, but you'll know what it really is—a bid to get him gloating before his team folds on the final play. Sucker!

The one exception to all of the above is when your clearly outmatched team starts running away with a game despite a long history of total ineptitude. In that case, call to gloat at every commercial break. You never know when you'll get another chance.

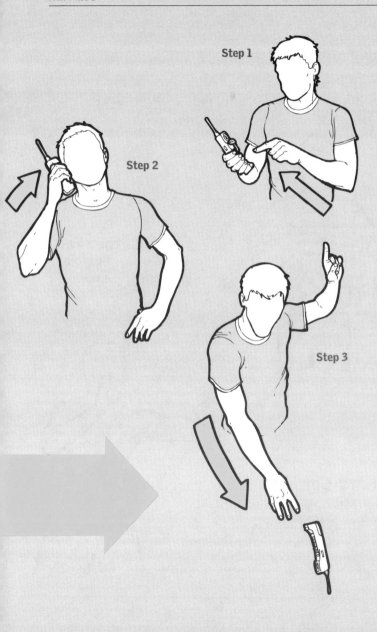

Step 1

Step 2

Step 3

How to Razz a Coach

If a bad coach just happens to work for your favorite team, that doesn't mean you can't heckle him. How far you're willing to go with your taunts says a lot about how serious you are as a fan.

Fair-Weather Fan
Hoists sign that's neither too insightful nor too intimidating.

Hard-Core Fan
Takes things to next level with a smart tattoo.

Psycho Fan

Currently serving three to five for mailing threatening letters to the coach's home because the team routinely fails to guard the pick-and-roll.

Christopher Noteboom

On November 27, 2005, during an Eagles-Packers game at Lincoln Field in Philadelphia, Noteboom, a Phoenix bar owner, ran onto the turf and dumped the ashes of his late mom, a rabid Eagles fan, on the 30-yard line.

His act set the standard for filial loyalty for decades to come, and gave new meaning to the phrase "three yards and a cloud of dust."

Magna Cum Loud: Sticking It to Nonsports Fans

You're a god when it comes to sports knowledge, but there are guys out there who just don't care. They'd rather spend their days reading the complete works of Dostoevsky, learning to fly planes, or becoming president of the United States—pretty much anything that doesn't involve reloading their team's online message board every four minutes. With all that extra time, nonfans do some interesting things, including advancing their careers and landing enviable sexual partners. No matter what they say, though, they secretly wish they knew about sports. Their lack of bar and watercooler banter burns them up inside. As a diehard fan, it's your job to make them feel small.

Here's How: Because a guy like that will do almost anything to fit in, he'll go along with what you say even if he has no freakin' clue what you're talking about. Bait his ignorance with false rumors like, "Can you believe the Pistons are considering signing Padraig Harrington?" Or "Did you hear the latest out of the boxing commissioner's office? Brian Boitano's going to have to surrender his belt."

Here's Another Good One: Buy a customized NBA jersey with the name Dumbass on the back. Make it a believable number, like 31. When the guy's birthday rolls around, give it to him as a gift. "Oh, you've never heard of Jerome Dumbass? The great power forward with the most unfortunate family lineage? This baby is instant street cred, bro. Wear it with pride." Coax him to try it on just to see if it fits, then begin yelling to everyone within earshot, "Hey, here comes the dumbass!" Just as quickly, lower your voice and say, "Just kidding. Happy birthday, bro! I love you. You know that, right?"

Dip Layers vs. Event Quality

The one vital component of every sports-viewing party: layered dip. How many layers? Good question. The final tally should be directly proportional to the magnitude of the event. For more info, consult this chart.

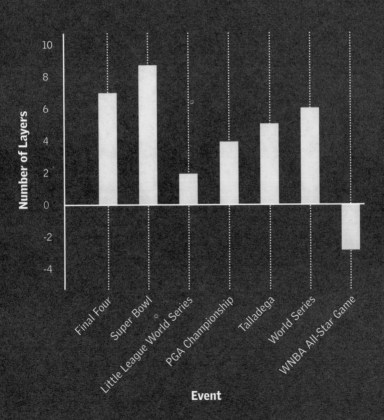

4

Chapter Four

Gambling and Fantasy Sports

Three Surefire Gambling Systems

1 Pick the team with your favorite jersey colors.

2 Bet on tips from your insider cousin (team trainer).

3 Use tip God gave you while you were at church.

Three Sure-Fail Gambling Systems

1 Pick the team with your favorite skin colors.

2 Bet on tips from your insider cousin (souvenir program vendor).

3 Use tip God gave you while you were at the bar.

Evading Your Bookie

At some point during your gambling career, you're going to find yourself in a very deep hole. The Sunday night game crapped out on you? Aw, nuts. Now you owe a bookie 45 grand—by Tuesday! Try one of these tactics.

➡️ It's clichéd, but true: Some bookies will still break the thumbs of a mark who won't pay up. But if you're already thumbless, the joke's on him, right? You can remove your thumbs using most any kitchen knife and a bit of moxie. If you do it right, it should be excruciatingly painful, so you might want to bite down on a stick or something. *[Note: If you've got more of a leg-breaking bookie, the same strategy applies, but you'll need a chain saw and help from a friend.]*

➡️ No bookie will have the stones to shake down a terror agent under constant federal surveillance. Make that reality work for you! Cruise the web for a militant fundamentalist message board and post something like, "I'm new here, but impressionable and angry. Anyone into crushing infidels?" You'll have two feds in Ray-Bans and Men's Wearhouse suits on your tail within the hour, and your bookie problem will be gone.

➡️ Wait for the bookie to bang on your door—then blow up the place. This isn't recommended as a first resort, as you'll be homeless. And dead.

Scott Harper

On August 9, 2005, Harper and three friends were watching a Yankees-White Sox game from the upper deck of Yankee Stadium when they began speculating about whether the netting behind home plate was strong enough to support a human body. Harper, an 18-year-old from Armonk, New York, decided to find out. He leapt 40 feet and landed safely on the net. Play was postponed until he could be removed, and a year later, a Bronx judge banned Harper from Yankee Stadium for life.

Pretty much everyone thinks he's a dumbass, but give Harper credit for answering the question drunk fans have pondered for ages. Can that net support the weight of a human being? Yes, it can!

The ABCs of Point-Shaving

If you know what you're doing, it's nearly impossible to lose money gambling. When you find yourself in a hole, don't bail like some run-of-the-mill OTB junkie. Try point-shaving! It couldn't be any simpler.

Ethical Digression No. 1: Find a college baller in need of a little extra cash. As long as the NCAA makes all the rules, this will be a snap. With the exception of the odd walk-on three-point specialist from the suburbs, everyone's exploited. Pro players are vulnerable to palm-greasing, too, but their services are often more expensive. Ditto referees.

Ethical Digression No. 2: Approach your mark after practice and offer to set him up with some "cheese on the side." He'll assume you're a corrupt booster or a Wendy's drive-through worker and go along. Tell him you'll give him $250 for every game he throws.

Ethical Digression No. 3: Call your bookie before each game, then sit and wait for the cabbage to roll in. See, this is the perfect crime. Everybody wins and nobody gets hurt. Unless, of course, organized crime or the federal government discovers what you've done.

Historical note: Teams with point-shaving pasts include Arizona State basketball, Peruvian national soccer, and the Washington Generals.

Rotisserie, Um, Chicken!
Hiding Your Fantasy Obsession

Yes indeed, nothing sucks you in quite as quickly or completely as fantasy sports. For most people, it begins with a phone call from a friend in need of an extra manager to fill out his league. You go along begrudgingly, even though "Stats don't tell the whole story" and "This is totally for nerds, dude." After the draft, your tune changes to something more like "Jesus Christ, if Jose Reyes doesn't start stealing bases, I'm going to drive to Queens and set his feet on fire!"

Still, most everyone who plays is vaguely ashamed of taking part in such a geekfest. As friends and clergymen can't be counted on to tolerate your fantasy life (that, of course, will always be the burden of your girlfriend), it's imperative to disguise your obsession at every turn. How?

⟶ Forget the following terms: "first-round value," "shallow mixed league," "keeper," "Rotisserie" (in any context other than poultry), and "big-play bonus." So people don't think you're a complete sociopath, you should also refrain from dropping the occasional, "What's the matter, TO? Bet you could catch a fist to the throat!"

⟶ Don't kid yourself. Where once you were invested in the performance of a favorite team, you're now preoccupied with every play, pass, and possession of every game played all season long. This is, in fact, physically impossible to maintain, so don't even try. If Lance Berkman needs one last RBI to win you the category for the week, bank on it. He's the RBI machine, you're the surgeon, and you need to stop that bleeding—"Suction!"—like, now.

⟶ When it comes to your favorite team vs. your fantasy team—say, the Eagles vs. the Giants—in a big-game situation, always side with your real-life favorite. A Philly loss may help you in the fantasy standings, but the charade of ditching your Eagles cap for an Eli Manning jersey will cause you untold pain and suffering. Celebrate your fantasy victory with a discreet fist-pump instead; it's the straight American male's stoic gesture of choice.

Don't talk about your fantasy team. Ever. To anybody. No one—except you—cares a whit about the middle-reliever strategy you used to stabilize your ERA and WHIP.

Finally, if winning truly is everything, you can hide your obsession and enhance your trade leverage by inviting your "friend" Frank to join the league before the season begins. Set up a Gmail account for Frank and draft him a good team. When you need, say, an extra outfielder or healthy running back, just have Frank send him your way. There, you've cheated, torpedoed your integrity, brought shame upon your family. And for what? The $200 league pool. Sounds like a bargain to us!

How to Rig Your League

The simplest way to win at fantasy anything is to start your own league—
and find a bunch of easy marks for the other manager slots. Ideally these
people don't know much about the sport at hand; they're signing on "you
know, just for the fun of it!" The great majority of nursing-home residents
make good competing managers, for example. Work this gambit right and
you'll end up with a draft in which everyone but you tries to take Ty Cobb
in the first round even after you've patiently explained that he's dead. Let
them take Cap Anson in the second round, though, if they think they can
win with him.

Overheard from Ideal Fantasy League Rivals

"Why can't I find Frank Gifford on this draft list?"
"I don't really watch sports, but let's make the buy-in a hundred bucks!"
"So I'm just going to draft white players this year ... "

Rules for Vetoing a Fantasy Trade

In most fantasy leagues, pending trades have to be reviewed by the
commissioner and all the team managers. Trades determined to be unfair
or collusive can be vetoed. Let us be clear: The only truly unfair or collusive
deals are the ones that don't involve your team. Veto all others promptly;
you'll need the spare time to plan your victory speech.

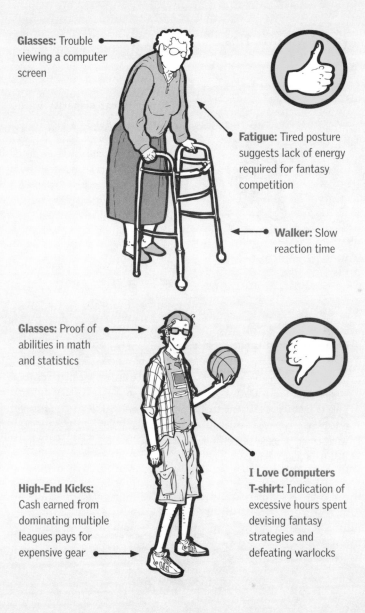

Glasses: Trouble viewing a computer screen

Fatigue: Tired posture suggests lack of energy required for fantasy competition

Walker: Slow reaction time

Glasses: Proof of abilities in math and statistics

High-End Kicks: Cash earned from dominating multiple leagues pays for expensive gear

I Love Computers T-shirt: Indication of excessive hours spent devising fantasy strategies and defeating warlocks

Fantasy Draft Tips

There is great disparity when it comes to fantasy league drafts. Every owner believes he or she has the never-fail formula, when in fact the entire thing is a random lottery. Invariably there will be first-round busts and undrafted players who end up as MVP material. It's simply impossible to tell what's going to happen before the season starts. Doesn't mean you can't intimidate and humiliate other owners.

Before the draft begins, print out a list of every player in the league. Make sure the names are small enough to fit on one side of an 8.5 x 11 sheet of paper. The more densely packed the names, the better. Walk around with this paper folded up in your pocket all day, flashing it from time to time while boasting to your fellow owners that this, your brilliant cheat sheet, has every round mapped out perfectly. "But how do you know what other people will pick?" they'll inquire. Just laugh and ask them if they're pretending to be stupid.

3

Once the draft begins, it's important to remain in the same room with the other owners. Otherwise they won't hear the muffled laughter you let slip after each and every pick. Every now and then, try adding condescending comments like "Are you serious?" or "Too late, you already said his name. I don't care if you were joking, now you're stuck with him." The great thing about the draft is that your rivals will invariably have to select some horrible players in rounds 15, 16, 17, and beyond. Feel free to dwell on those selections. "I've heard of sleeper picks, but your entire team is hibernating. Why not throw your buy-in into a wastepaper basket? It'll save you time."

When the other owners defend themselves by claiming that this is just a friendly league, and that while they've never met you before, they needed a tenth to round everything out and you were recommended by a friend of a friend, don't listen to them. These guys are your mortal enemies. Treat them as such and you will do fine.

5

Chapter Five

Love, Work, and Other Hindrances

The Reeses

Hardcore Alabama fans Freeman and Betty Reese skipped their own daughter's wedding to attend the Crimson Tide-Tennessee game. "You know we made the reception," Freeman later explained. "Drove to it straight from the ball game."

Their act of defiance earned them the admiration of millions of football fans, and prompted thousands to ask: "Why was the daughter getting married during the Bama-Tennessee game?"

Bailing: The Science of Dodging Responsibilities and Other Impediments to the Enjoyment of Sports

Life often interferes with sports. Hard though it might be to maneuver through the changing seasons—baseball into football, football into basketball, etc.—the challenge is only compounded when other, lesser factors intrude (i.e., household chores, office deadlines, a certain someone known as your spouse). If you're not careful, the three-headed beast of family, friends, and job can devour a well-orchestrated weekend of essential sports viewing. No sports fan deserves this, but thousands die such small deaths each day, watching in desperation as millions of perfectly useful couch hours get tossed in the wood chipper. The key to avoiding the unthinkable? Prevention and planning.

❶ MAKE PLANS

They don't have to make sense. In fact, they don't even have to include specific details, since those only invite the scrutiny of bosses and wives. Just make plans ahead of time, months and years ahead of time. Unbreakable plans.

> **Your Wife:** "Saturday we're going antiquing with Maggie and Todd."

> **You:** "Ooh, honey, sorry. I'm helping needy kids learn how to swim down at the Y."

Your Wife: "How noble! Can I help?"

You: "No, they're suspicious of strangers, and they scare easily. Better let me handle it."

On Saturday, proceed directly to your favorite sports bar with the ringer on your cell firmly in the off position.

② CREATE FALSE IDENTITIES AND JOBS

Which presents a more persuasive case? "I'm missing the christening because of the game," or "My activities on Sunday are a matter of national security. If you need me, call this number and ask for 'Ahmed.' "

Be sure to recruit a trustworthy friend to be "Ahmed."

③ BLAME IT ON THE KIDS

Turning the tables on your opponent is a gutsy move. However, nothing says male ritual quite like taking your kid to his first game. For extra emphasis, be sure to drop in words and phrases like "bonding," "tradition," "fatherhood," and "quality time."

> **Important Reminder!** Be sure to bring the kid to the game, as the illusion will be shattered if he or she is left weeping at the front door.

④ BAIL

....

A simple but effective technique when all else fails.

....

STEP 1: Hide. Behind a large couch is ideal, but cabinets, invisibility cloaks, wardrobes, and even large houseplants will do in a pinch. Choose a spot beyond the customary route of your spouse and wait until she advances deep into the house.

STEP 2: Sprint to freedom!

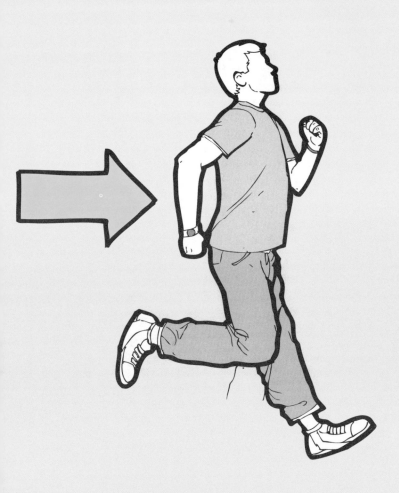

A Psycho Fan's Guide to Child Rearing

For so-called normal people, the birth of a child is a time to rejoice and celebrate the miracle of life. For the hard-core sports fan, having a kid can be a source of extreme anxiety. From the moment the doctor snips the umbilical cord and wipes that gunk off Junior's face, you've got at best six years to make sure the little guy doesn't start pulling for the wrong team. The clock is ticking. A few helpful suggestions:

1 **Name the kid after your coach** Nothing brainwashes a child quite like forcing him or her to bear the name of your team's head coach. According to psychologists, this creates a powerful sense of identification, which means rooting against the coach (and by proxy, your team) would be like rooting against oneself. Borderline personality disorder, bed-wetting, depression, etc., may result. Talk about incentive.

2 **Play the fight song incessantly in Junior's crib** During those crucial first few months, your newborn's neurons are rapidly forming connections. Why not use them to guarantee team allegiance for decades to come? Painting baby's room in team colors and crowding the crib with stuffed team mascots is also effective.

3 **Demonize kids whose parents like other teams** Few things are as important to your child's development as the people who surround him. Fans of other teams will go to incredible lengths to recruit little Billy into their "lifestyle." Teach him never to take candy from or get into a car with these perverts.

4 **Use reverse psychology** *(Recommended for children age 2 and older.)* Many kids flirt with the idea that they're free to choose their favorite team. If your child shows signs of developing such an independent streak, do not get angry. Try what scientists call reverse psychology, a powerful technique employed by military interrogators. If young Sally expresses affection for a rival, you might say, "That's okay, you weren't worthy of pulling for my team, anyway." Or "No problem. I always knew you didn't have it in you." Then let her think about it for a while. This will work nine times out of 10. Failing that, go to rule No. 5.

5 Threaten disinheritance Most 6-year-olds don't know the vagaries of estate law, but now's as good a time as any to teach them. Simulate the act of disinheritance by taking all of your disobedient child's toys, giving them to a sibling, and saying, "See? Pull for the other team, and your little sister will get all this while you get nothing."

6 Play the Santa card For the truly hard-core cases, see to it that the fat man doesn't bring any gifts on Christmas Day. Leave a team-specific note under the tree instead:

> Sorry, kids, but I can't in good conscience shower gifts on Auburn fans. That's most certainly naughty. Roll Tide!
>
> Love, Santa

Sure, you might feel you've gone a tad too far when you see those disappointed little faces, but to be a good parent sometimes means being the bad guy. Besides, with the money you've saved on toys, you can buy yourself Super Bowl tickets.

Building a Home Shrine to Your Team

Any fan can paint a rec room in his team's colors, hang up a pennant or two and a framed panoramic fish-eye-lens photograph of his favorite stadium, and call it a shrine. But a proper shrine, the kind that makes other fans say, "Holy crap, you're crazy," requires special planning and a few must-have elements.

 Wall of Jock Straps

Few things say, "I support my team" like a wall of used, sweat-stained athletic supporters. Arrange symmetrically or in an arc over a sofa. Hang au natural, rather than framed, to facilitate easy sniffing and passing around to friends.

 Athlete's Foot Farm

A simple swab and a petri dish are all you need to culture and grow a flourishing colony of aromatic fungus from the damp floor of your favorite team's shower room. Collectors especially prize fungus that can be traced to the sole of a specific player's foot, so if you can pull that off without getting pummeled by an offended athlete, more power to you. If kept in a humid aquarium and mowed from time to time, it will last for years.

 Multiple Plasma TVs

Anyone can watch highlights of a favorite game. But can you watch highlights of eight or ten favorite games at once? No? Well then, get your butt down to Best Buy! Ask for Terry, and tell him you want the "discount."

 Marble Reliquary of Favorite Athlete's Nail Clippings

An excellent centerpiece for any collection. Touching before game time is widely believed to increase chances of winning by 10–15%.

Live Mascot Petting Zoo

Like the Eagles? Get some eagles!! A large, netted flyway and some scraps of raw rodent meat are all you need for this eye-catching addition to your fan shrine. Same deal if you like the Lions, Tigers, or Bears, but you'll probably need a bit more rodent meat. Careful around the kids.

 Dip Bowl, Napkins, Extra Batteries for the Remote, Duct Tape, Bailing Twine

When going out on a limb, don't forget the basics.

. . . .

Tips for Getting Started

1 It's best to assemble your fan shrine when your spouse is out of town. This will give you plenty of time to implement architectural and design changes that will be all but impossible to undo.

2 Use credit cards to buy overpriced memorabilia. Credit cards are a practically endless source of cash, which can come in handy when the bidding gets heady on eBay. Helpful, too, when smuggling in panthers, lions, and other hard-to-find mascots.

3 Befriend or bribe a locker room attendant. These guys have access to sweat bands, used towels, and undergarments that nicely compliment any fan shrine.

4 Invest in a security system. Jealous fans might try to steal your stuff. Alarms, electric fences, and automated poison dart guns will deter even the most covetous among them, not to mention a rival or two hell-bent on vandalizing your collection. Hint: A taxidermied rival fan looks great near the bar!

Proposing at Halftime: A Vow That Wows

One day, you'll find someone more important to you than any game—a love that transcends your passion for the team. And when you find that perfect woman, you will buy her the perfect ring. What comes next? The perfect JumboTron.

Yes, nothing says romance like 20,000 anonymous fans scrutinizing your every pore moments after the public address announcer pops the question.

A halftime proposal is wonderful for so many reasons. First, it combines the two things you love most in the world: sports and expensive fast food. Second, you can forget the candles; everybody knows there is no glow more alluring than arena lighting. And last but not least, a woman is far less likely to say no with 20,000 people watching.

SPECIAL BONUS: A Sweet-Nothing Suggestion

....

"Go get us some hot dogs, wouldya baby? I don't wanna miss a second of this wonderful experience. Hey, can you believe we're engaged?"

....

Effective Taunting for Pee Wee League Slackers

Even world-class motivators aren't afraid to lay down a good taunt if they think it will help propel a team of 9-year-olds to victory.

SOME EXCELLENT EXAMPLES:

- "Make this free throw or I'm divorcing your mother!"

- "That's it! One more strikeout and you're going to the orphanage!"

- "Your brother we abandoned in the woods would have made that shot."

- "You'll look hungrier next game if we stop feeding you!"

- "Sloppy play like that is what made the dog run away!"

Mark Roberts

The world's all-time leading streaker. Since first baring it all at the Rugby Sevens matches in Hong Kong in 1993, Roberts, 43, has streaked at more than 380 sports events, including Super Bowl XXXVIII, where he snuck onto the field disguised as a referee.

What can you say? Dude just loves running around buck naked in front of thousands of strangers at sporting events.

Listening to the Game at School Plays, Weddings, Funerals, and Other Nuisances: An Illustrated Tactical Guide

THE INTELLECTUAL

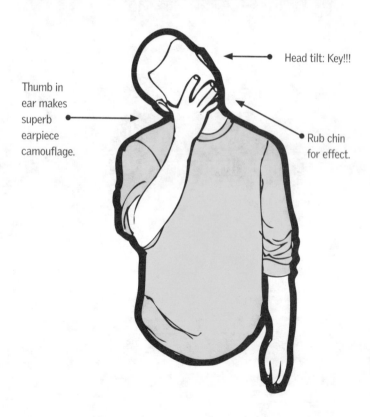

Head tilt: Key!!!

Thumb in ear makes superb earpiece camouflage.

Rub chin for effect.

CHILLIN'

Say hi without saying hi with the finger point.

Wall: A must-have!!!

Devil-may-care expression.

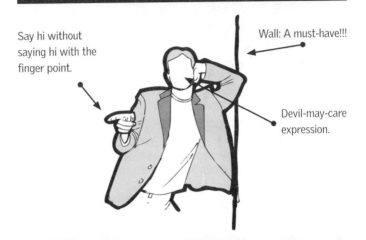

THE SIAMESE TWIN

Tender moment? Or two fans splitting one earpiece? They'll never know with a well-executed move like this.

LA ROMANTIQUE

In love,
with sports.

Overcome with emotion? Sure, but they'll never know
the real reason why ...

THE HALLELUJAH COVER

Hallelujah!
Amen!
Hallelujah!

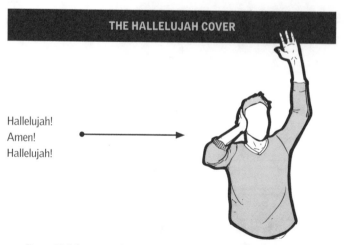

Essential for covering positive, uncontrollable outbursts of
joy after scores, turnovers, or any stroke of good luck.

NOT AFRAID TO CRY

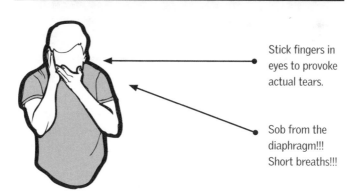

Stick fingers in eyes to provoke actual tears.

Sob from the diaphragm!!! Short breaths!!!

THE CRYIN' SHOULDER

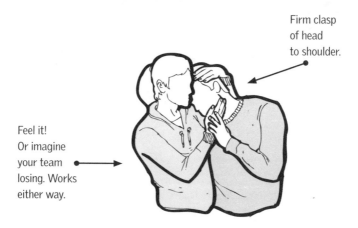

Firm clasp of head to shoulder.

Feel it! Or imagine your team losing. Works either way.

THE 911

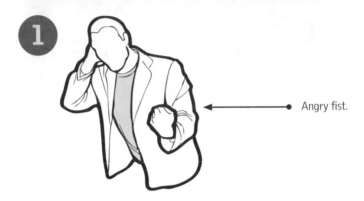

Angry fist.

Cover blown? Not so fast! A quick clutch of the chest turns a potential breach of etiquette into a face-saving medical emergency!!!

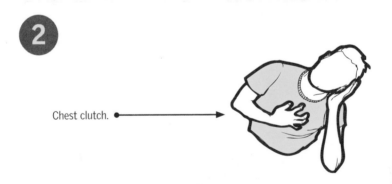

Chest clutch.

Panic! Actually, if your team just lost, you should look like this anyway. Still, sell it!

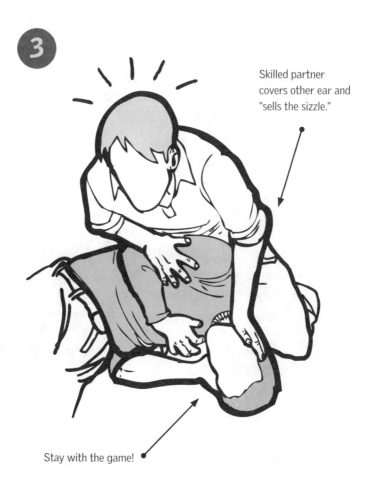

3

Skilled partner covers other ear and "sells the sizzle."

Stay with the game!

Chapter Six

Between Games

Avoiding the Score: The Art of the Tape Delay

There will come a day when something prevents you from watching the game at the appropriate start time. Thankfully, due to recent technological innovation, it's now possible to watch your favorite team whenever you want. The only problem: how to avoid hearing the final score.

The thing to remember is that you can't hear or see a final score when you don't hear or see anything. Until you're safe at home in front of the TV, you want to limit your senses to three: touch, smell, and taste. This is because it's physically impossible to touch, smell, or taste the final score of a game.

Let's say you're obliged to attend an important funeral, one that you simply can't avoid (blood relative or closer). Even if you bail early, you're going to miss the first half. So you tape the game, and drive home in a hurry. Common sense requires that you avoid listening to the radio along the way. But if you want to play it really, really safe, you should probably blindfold yourself and stuff your ears with a very dense gauze so that nobody can yell or text message you the score while you drive.

Sense the roads to your house, then get out of the car and crawl toward the television set. As you reach the TV on hands and knees, remove the blindfold and ear gauze and hit play. "Funny, I don't remember my house being in the middle of this cornfield, but that's where I ended up."

Game time, baby!

Appraising Your Memorabilia Collection: A Flowchart

Think your memorabilia collection's pretty swanky?
See where your items fit in on our hierarchy, presented here in ascending order of intrinsic value:

11. AUTOGRAPH ACQUIRED AT CARD SHOW

10. AUTOGRAPH ACQUIRED AT TEAM HOTEL

9. FOUL BALL CAUGHT AT STADIUM

8. HOME RUN BALL CAUGHT AT STADIUM

7. BROKEN BAT

6. BAT USED TO HIT HOME RUN

5. GAME-WORN JERSEY

4. LOCK OF PLAYER'S HAIR

3. PLAYER'S UNEXPIRED CREDIT CARD

2. PLAYER'S APPENDIX REMOVED BEFORE GAME 7 OF WORLD SERIES

1. PLAYER'S CRYOGENICALLY PRESERVED HEAD IN REALLY SWEET LUCITE DISPLAY CASE

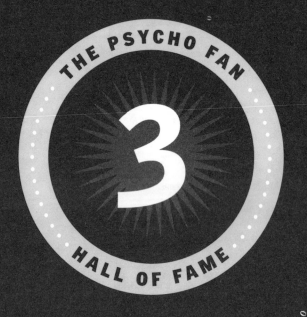

Eric James Torpy

In 2005 prosecutors offered a 30-year sentence to the diehard Celtics fan in exchange for a guilty plea to robbery and shooting with intent to kill. Torpy threatened to reject the deal unless the Oklahoma City court tacked on three more years to match the number of his favorite Celtic, Larry Bird (#33). The judge accommodated him.

Today, Torpy sits in his cell kicking himself for not telling the judge his favorite Celtic was really Robert Parish (#00).

Dominating the (Internet Message) Boards

Rule 1: Choose a Name Carefully Be slightly creative, but not too creative. Several formulas have demonstrated tried-and-true success. Among them:

➤ [Team] + "fan" + [fan's year of birth or last championship] yields, for example, CELTICSFAN84

➤ A pun based on the name of a favorite player or coach. The possibilities are limitless: "THEPHILJACKSON5," "MOOKIE BLAYLOCKJAW," "PUJOLSIN1," "THE RANDYMOSSTRICH," "WOODCHIPPERJONES," "HONKYTONK BADONKAPRONK," etc.

Rule 2: State Opinions Violently This begins, of course, with actually having an opinion. If you're the second to post a message, disagree with the first. Obey this rule (and all those that follow) always. Whether or not you believe in what you're saying is immaterial.

Rule 3: Support Is a Brand of Panty Hose When arguing with someone, provide no backup whatsoever for your opinion. Instead, assault your opponent's manhood, character, and education (or lack thereof). If all else fails, assail his spelling or misuse of punctuation. "Like I can believe your opinions on the 2-3 zone—you can't even defend yourself against the improper use of a semicolon!"

Rule 4: Never Surrender Just because most everyone else has given up on your debate over the greatest NBA player named Earl doesn't mean you have to, Mr. Lincoln. The last word wins even if it comes on page 238 of the thread.

Rule 5: When in Doubt, Claim You Know Someone Important Even
the trainer's third-cousin, Eddie, who just got out of jail for mail fraud,
can be considered a primary source for message board rumors. Refer
to him like Deep Throat in your arguments, and never, ever doubt his
credibility.

Rule 6: Fire the Coach Any and all problems in sports can be ascribed to
the clear and evident failings of your coach. He must be dispatched now, if
not sooner.

It's great to find a platform to air your opinions on stolen bases. However, that microphone's for karaoke, and you're really killing this party.

Sports Radio Call-In Shows: A Fail-Safe Formula for Phoning It In

It can be tough to find a broad audience for your semicoherent ramblings, but have no fear—you too can join the cavalcade of screaming talk radio callers. Trust us: Screeners for sports call-in shows aren't looking for creativity. They want overheated, larynx-shredding opinion, preferably on completely inconsequential topics. There's a formula (below). Follow it and you're golden for a full 30 seconds of local radio fame. Don't laugh—this is how Howard Cosell got his start.

"HI, I'M A FIRST-TIME CALLER"

Hey, what's up, (hosts' names)?! I've loved (show's name) for forever, dude! Anyway, my question is, do you think (player's name) is going to play worse now that he's been indicted for (name of a felony)? See, (overly familiar shortening of a host's name), I think he's going to come out strong and really want to prove everyone wrong. It's like in (year prior to your birth), when (obscure historical player) scored (some very high number) while carrying a (name of animal) on his (body part). You guys remember that? And (historical team name) won the pennant that year, even with half of the team battling (drug that hasn't been abused since 1920) addiction.

Yeah, and if the team still struggles, it's time to fire (coach's name). I mean, can you imagine if we replaced him with (out-of-work disgraced coach's name)? It's a win-win deal! But don't let me complain, I (bodily function) (team color). Go (team name)!

How to Meet Athletes

Getting a chance to meet your favorite sports heroes doesn't have to be a hobby. The resourceful Psycho Fan can make it his job, too.

Job: Bail Bondsman

Pros: You get to carry a gun.

Cons: You'll eventually have to meet Stephen Jackson.

Job: Memorabilia Seller

Pros: Are you good at standing in line to get autographs? Then this is the life for you!

Cons: No memorabilia seller in the history of the memorabilia industry has ever had sex with a woman. And there haven't been any close calls, either.

Job: Posse Member

Pros: Free food, free car, and sitting around playing video games all day can be yours if you can stand behind a belligerent NBA star and say, "Uh-huh!" and "That's right!"

Cons: The player takes one trip to the D-League and you're eating macaroni for the rest of your life. Plus, like British royalty, you have to be born into it.

Job: Coach

....

Pros: You get a huge salary and the best seat in the house for every game.

....

Cons: After Little League, telling everyone to try their best doesn't qualify as coaching. Offering to buy the team ice cream if they win won't snap a losing streak.

Job: Benchwarmer

....

Pros: You get your own baseball card. So what if it ends up on the spokes of some kid's bicycle?

....

Cons: You will be mercilessly mocked by schoolchildren, the elderly, and your immediate family.

Signature Moves: Mastering the Autograph Hunt

Sure, you can watch every game, wear your replica jersey to church, and have your favorite player's number tattooed on your back, but you're not a true fan until you have that indelible mark of your obsession: an autograph. If you're thinking that there's no way a hastily scribbled signature on a baseball could be more valuable than a mother's love, then your trembling hands have never handed a Sharpie to a career platoon player and said, "Can you sign it 'Keep swinging for the fences, champ'?"

With the proper grit and determination, an aspiring autograph-seeker can get the kind of precious heirloom that sits on a mantel and makes visitors utter, "Hmmm ... you say he used to play for the Cardinals?" in bemused jealousy for years to come.

TIP: Seem just sad enough, but not pathetic Athletes are busy people, but if it looks like they'll save your week, you can usually get them to stop and sign. The trick here is to seem moderately pitiful, but not needy or creepy. To get into the right semi-sad frame of mind, you might want to think about the death of a pet, but not one that you liked too much. For extra attention, say, "Oh, man, this is the best moment of my life, but I'm sure the day I finally move out of my parents' house will be even better."

TIP: Never ask for more than one signature You want to give the impression that you're looking for a treasure for your desk, not something to run home and immediately throw on eBay. Since you're only getting one signature, make sure to pick the item you want signed carefully to ensure its appropriateness for the player in question. Granted, an autographed football is pretty cool, but Dominique Wilkins just didn't have the breakaway speed to make it in the NFL.

TIP: Never, ever give up. As long as your favorite player is alive, there's no excuse for not getting his or her autograph Doggedly pursue your goal, even if that includes going onto private property or hiding in the closet of his or her hotel room. If you begin to lose your resolve, remind yourself that a signed restraining order is not only an autograph, it's also notarized.

Purists balk at the idea of approaching an athlete while he's eating. Don't let anyone tell you this is rude. Any player who gets paid to scratch himself on national television is hardly in a position to give you a lecture on the finer points of good manners.

TIP: Card conventions are for quitters Most athletes appear several times a year at sports-card or memorabilia conventions and, for a small fee, sign any item put before them. In much the same way strippers are a poor substitute for actual naked girls, these encounters will leave you ultimately unsatisfied. Instead, seek out your target at the team hotel during road trips, entering the park or arena on game day, in the locker room shower following the game, or at his next arraignment. We could go on, but we have to get back to Ryan Howard's house. He takes out the trash at 9:42 most Tuesday nights, and this time, we'll be there.

A tattoo of a player's signature is the autograph that lasts forever. Exercise caution, though, as few athletes are competent tattoo artists.

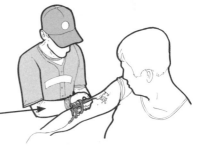

Understanding Your Head Coach

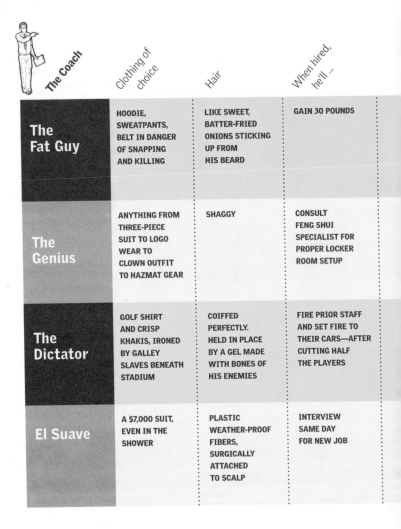

The Coach	Clothing of choice	Hair	When hired, he'll ...
The Fat Guy	HOODIE, SWEATPANTS, BELT IN DANGER OF SNAPPING AND KILLING	LIKE SWEET, BATTER-FRIED ONIONS STICKING UP FROM HIS BEARD	GAIN 30 POUNDS
The Genius	ANYTHING FROM THREE-PIECE SUIT TO LOGO WEAR TO CLOWN OUTFIT TO HAZMAT GEAR	SHAGGY	CONSULT FENG SHUI SPECIALIST FOR PROPER LOCKER ROOM SETUP
The Dictator	GOLF SHIRT AND CRISP KHAKIS, IRONED BY GALLEY SLAVES BENEATH STADIUM	COIFFED PERFECTLY. HELD IN PLACE BY A GEL MADE WITH BONES OF HIS ENEMIES	FIRE PRIOR STAFF AND SET FIRE TO THEIR CARS—AFTER CUTTING HALF THE PLAYERS
El Suave	A $7,000 SUIT, EVEN IN THE SHOWER	PLASTIC WEATHER-PROOF FIBERS, SURGICALLY ATTACHED TO SCALP	INTERVIEW SAME DAY FOR NEW JOB

His secretary ...	When plays go wrong, he ...	When fired, he'll ...	In an alternate reality, he would ...
HAS DOMINO'S ON SPEED DIAL AND KNOWS CPR	THROWS THINGS, FRIGHTENS CARDIOLOGIST	WEEP... INTO HIS CHEESE FRIES	SURVIVE FAMINES BY KILLING AND EATING LESSER MEN
NEEDS TRANSLATORS AND RESEARCH ASSISTANT TO PROCESS SIMPLE REQUESTS	STARES BEMUSED INTO DISTANCE, BECAUSE HE HAS ALREADY FORESEEN THIS	GO TO INDIA FOR SIX MONTHS, THEN RESURFACE IN L.A. AS A NAKED YOGI	DESIGN SINISTER WEAPONS FOR FEDS OR LIVE UNDER A BRIDGE. POSSIBLY BOTH
FLEES COUNTRY AFTER TWO WEEKS TO UNDISCLOSED DESTINATION	THINKS ONLY ABOUT MURDER. SWEET, SWEET MURDER	TAKE GIG AS TV ANALYST, KICK PUPPIES FOR FUN IN SPARE TIME	SEE HIS ENEMIES DRIVEN BEFORE HIM, AND HEAR THE LAMENTATIONS OF THEIR WOMEN
BEARS SEVERAL OF HIS CHILDREN OUT OF WEDLOCK	SCANS STANDS FOR FUTURE MISTRESSES, CALLS AGENT	ALREADY HAVE ANOTHER JOB LINED UP, NOT TO MENTION CHILD SUPPORT PAYMENTS FOR NEW SECRETARY ARRANGED	BE HANGED AT SEA FOR TREASON

The Boxer's Entourage and You

Boxing is an age-old sport pitting man against man in the most primitive of contests. It also poses challenges for the Psycho Fan because of the expense involved in attending: The average fight ticket now costs $36,578 for nosebleeds. Ringside tickets require payment arrangements involving solid bars of platinum or firstborn children, sometimes both. Do not let this discourage you. Even if you cannot afford the privilege of being splattered by the blood of guys who were expelled from preschool, boxing still affords opportunities for the average Psycho Fan. The best of these? Becoming a member of a boxing entourage. Ways to join one include the following:

1 Become a Hanger-On Posse membership is relatively easy. Either arrange to be born close to a professional boxer and befriend him in childhood or be related to him. An alternate route is to commit a noncapital felony and hope you're put in the same cellblock.

2 Become a Cut Man Deep bruises to the face necessitate the employment of a cut man. His job is to lash the boxer on the face with a razor without rhyme or reason, then apply tiny Band-Aids to taco-size wounds. This requires only bravery, as cut men are widely considered to be the rodeo clowns of the boxing world.

3 Become His Manager This is the easiest route to insider status, and if you're a convicted murderer, all the better! The manager has three simple responsibilities: steal, schedule fights, and steal. Take whatever a boxer earns in a bout and subtract $38—this is the fighter's cut. The rest is yours, which you should quickly wire to a shadowy investment fund in Bermuda or Nauru.

Presto! Just like that, you're a boxing insider!

All hangers-on carry the same responsibility in a fight:
Shove someone and yell, "WHAT? WHAT? HUH? WHAT?" Should
someone fall on the ground, stomp your foot next to the individual's head,
and continue screaming the fight mantra.

Chapter Seven

Advanced
Techniques

Streaking

Streaking requires no equipment and has no rules, save one: that you be naked where others are clothed. All the aspiring streaker needs is an audience and a means for sneaking into an arena where he will be seen. The following strategies will give you the mental edge you need to make your ass as recognizable as the Taj Mahal or the Mona Lisa.

THE BASICS

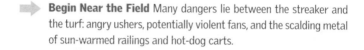

Begin Near the Field Many dangers lie between the streaker and the turf: angry ushers, potentially violent fans, and the scalding metal of sun-warmed railings and hot-dog carts.

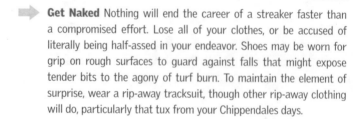

Get Naked Nothing will end the career of a streaker faster than a compromised effort. Lose all of your clothes, or be accused of literally being half-assed in your endeavor. Shoes may be worn for grip on rough surfaces to guard against falls that might expose tender bits to the agony of turf burn. To maintain the element of surprise, wear a rip-away tracksuit, though other rip-away clothing will do, particularly that tux from your Chippendales days.

Ready ... Set ... Go! A Clean Entry Is Essential Timing is overrated, but wait for a lull to minimize the chances of hurting your team. Locate TV cameras for maximum exposure, find an open running lane, and ... hang it out there!

PRE-STREAK PLANNING

To help with the inevitable legal expenses, secure an endorsement from an online casino before you streak. The exposure gained from a temporary tattoo on your posterior advertising the name and number of a law firm should cover the fee of a marginally competent lawyer. If no sponsor is available, find a friend who will wager a substantial sum on the likelihood of you chickening out, then prove him wrong.

CAVEAT STREAKER

Beginning streakers are strenuously discouraged from selecting for their maiden runs the following sports as they are of the highest difficulty:

Rodeo	Paintball	Motorsports (all)
Bobsled	Luge	Boxing
Steeplechase	Javelin	Hammer Toss
Horse Racing	Bearbaiting	Competitive Skiing

Scientists have noted that most streakers trace a path that looks like the Olympic rings. The same scientists still aren't sure why they're studying streakers.

DURING THE RUN:

For Accomplished Streakers Only

The Gait Head high, knees up—like an ostrich running for its life, but with less plumage. Look over your shoulder frequently to gauge security personnel's pursuit angles.

The Sun Salutation If pursuit and time allow, face the crowd, spread your arms, and say hello. If it won't slow you down too much, blow the crowd some kisses, as you are their hero.

The Exit Plan There isn't one. If you're fortunate, you'll be gently leveled by security. But odds are you won't be so lucky, in which case it's a good idea to appease the angry police dog with your nonwriting arm. Also, just saying "No Taser can stop me!" doesn't make it true.

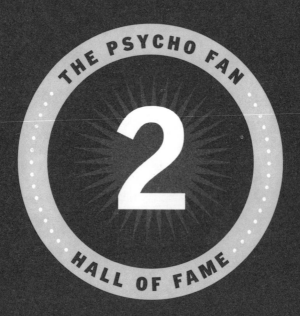

THE PSYCHO FAN

2

HALL OF FAME

James Henry Smith

At the funeral home after his death, Smith, a lifelong Steelers fan, was placed in a recliner, beer and cigarettes at his side, remote clutched in his right hand, facing a TV that played a video of classic Steelers highlights.

Say, Jim, do you mind switching over to the Cowboys game for a sec? Oh—*sorry!*

How to Tear Down a Goalpost

Tearing down a goalpost is an excellent way to celebrate a big victory. It's also a great way to get killed and/or paralyzed for life. Fortunately for people enthralled by scenes of mob violence and mayhem, that's not much of a deterrent to today's college kids. Here are a few constructive tips:

1 Before you storm the field, make sure your team has actually won. If you storm the field after the other team has won, highlights of you idiotically racing out to celebrate a loss will be replayed on sports television for years to come.

. . . .

2 If you're sure your side has won, then get on out there! No fence, no problem—simply run like hell. If there's a fence, you'll need to scale it. A member of your group should help catapult the others over the barrier. (This is a thankless and tiring job, so designate someone else to do it.) Have him perfect a heaving action, then repeat it approximately 15 to 20,000 times, or until the student section is empty.

. . . .

3 Once on the field, you'll want to make a beeline for the goalpost. Dozens, perhaps hundreds, of police officers will try to thwart you in this effort. Avoid them.

. . . .

4 If you manage to make it past the billy clubs, the pepper spray, and the high-voltage dart guns, you're well on your way to tearing down a goalpost. Now you must mount the actual post itself. You may either shimmy up the center post, or get on your pals' shoulders and reach for the crossbar. Once on the bar, you'll need to bounce and twist in an exaggerated fashion. You might be on TV at this moment, so smile.

5 At some point, your celebration will be interrupted by a violent snap, followed perhaps by a free fall, tumbling bodies, and cries for help. This is a good reason not to hang out directly under the crossbar. If the goalpost in question is made of steel, you might need to enlist the help of some engineering students. They'll probably be drunk out of their minds and happy to help you, as engineering students have no friends.

FUN FACT: Goalposts cost $6,000 each—but not your $6,000.

SIC TRANSIT GLORIA MUNDI

Tearing down goalposts might one day become a thing of the past. Several universities have installed so-called hinged goalposts, which automatically lower near the end of a game so that they can't be needlessly destroyed. While this doesn't bode well for the tearing down of goalposts over the long haul, most universities (fortunately) are simply too cheap to make the change right now. And, technically anyway, there's nothing to prevent you from picking up a goalpost that's been lowered for safety reasons, lifting it in the air, and tearing it down again.

Camping Out for Tickets: A Packing List

The true undergraduate fan will go to any length to get choice seats for a big game, so the ticket campout has become a venerable tradition. Unlike a Boy Scout camping trip, there's little you need to bring.

THE BASIC REQUIREMENTS:

A blatant disregard for what camping out for three weeks in freezing temperatures will do to your grades and your personal health.

A sleeping bag (optional).

That's pretty much it, although you might want to stop along the way and pick up some beer and wings.

How to Torch a Sofa

If you really want to celebrate your school's big win in style, there's only one way to go: Torch a sofa in a public thoroughfare. Because appropriate moments to do so typically arise immediately before full-scale riots erupt, you'll need to act quickly, lest you miss out on the looting. There's not much to it. Find a sofa, lug it to the site, douse it in kerosene, and apply a flame to any or all of the flash points in this diagram.

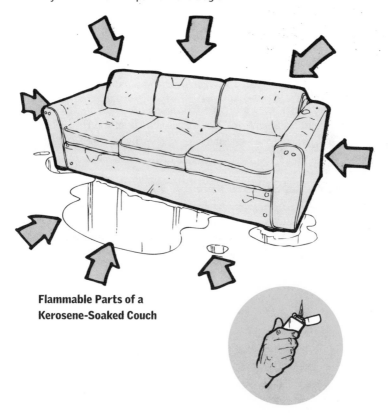

Flammable Parts of a Kerosene-Soaked Couch

How to Kidnap a Mascot

When you're playing a hated rival, you need to exploit every advantage. The starting point guard's father is in prison? Make a hilarious sign about it. That Pac-10 tailback flunked remedial math and had to sit out a game? Try a scathing cheer, say, "2-4-6-8—you don't know what those numbers add up to, stupid!" (Should anyone ask, the answer is probably 20.)

It's tougher to torment your rivals when you're playing on the road. After all, how do you compete with thousands of screaming fans? By silencing them. With extreme prejudice. How? By kidnapping their mascot. Two pointers:

If the Mascot Is a Live Animal Bulldogs, falcons, severely confused cattle—almost any living animal can be made into a team icon. Fortunately, they're usually docile and—excepting the cattle—easy to swipe. Fleet feet and a burlap sack will do.

Once You've Got the Critter Home Here your choices get tougher. It's your call, really: Lovingly care for the beast, or pass it through a meat grinder, then sell the wurst to tailgaters as Official Rival U. Sausages. If anyone acts wise, tell them the mustard's on the house. Then run as fast as you can.

If the Mascot Is a Person Same as above, except you'll need an ether rag.

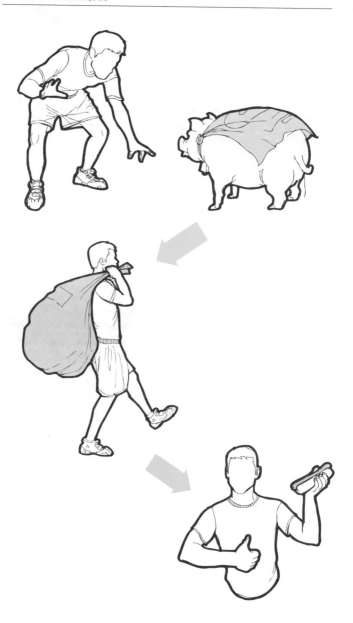

Fan Funerals for Your Consideration

The Fair-Weather Fan...

is buried in a casket with the team logo on it.

The Hard-Core Fan...

has a loved one spread his ashes on the field during a game.

The Psycho Fan...

has his ashes mixed with the team's Gatorade so he can really "get into the game for once."

When Athletes Attack!

In successfully employing the strategies meticulously outlined in this book, you might go too far in your adulation. At that point, a very large man is going to want to remove your head with a Gatorade bucket. Remember these lifesaving steps:

1 Get into the fetal position.

....

2 Take a shot at his groin when, between blows, he stops to catch his breath.

....

3 Run like hell.

....

4 Call your lawyer. You're about to get a fat out-of-court settlement, stud!

....

5 Use part of your windfall to buy season tickets so you can cheer on the player who assaulted you. Remember: Real fans—even the most fantastically psycho ones—forgive.

The family may laugh at you when you take gas masks to every game, but when the tear gas starts flying, they'll literally come crawling back.

Scrums and Full-Blown Riots: Making It Out Alive

Yours is not to reason why, yours is simply not to die. Here are a few helpful tips for surviving a riot:

- Clothing is extremely important. Stay close to people whose team shirts match yours. Avoid those whose don't. If you can't tell, the solution is simple: Kick that person in the groin and run.

- Tear gas can be your friend. If you find yourself about to take a brutal beating, run toward that noxious cloud. Should anyone want to follow you in to give you a stomping, well, they've earned it.

- Pull out your wallet and hold it unfolded, like a police badge, in front of you to clear a path through the crowd. If one's available, use a friend as an "arrested suspect." If someone asks you what he's charged with, say "Sassin' an officer, boy. You wanna be next?"

- As mounted police take the field, start an impromptu betting pool with bystanders on which horse will cross midfield first. Try to earn some extra cheddar by betting a high-risk exacta.

- As always, wear sunscreen.

Player Stalking
(a.k.a. Aggressive Friendship Courting)

Stalking exes can be tough. They switch apartments without telling you, drive inconspicuous Hondas, and take out restraining orders that their lawyers just won't shut up about when you finally get some face time in court. It can be a real hassle and often isn't worth the trouble.

Your favorite athlete, though—he's a piece of cake!

Doesn't he seem so cool and laid-back whenever you see him interviewed on TV? Man, you guys would totally hit it off! Maybe even be best friends. He'd even let you see the 50-inch plasma screen in his game room, where he plays Xbox.

Yeah, that would be sweet!

But first you've got to get to know him, and since he's an athlete, stalking him will be a breeze. In fact, it's so easy let's not even call it stalking; it's more like "aggressive friendship courting."

The great thing about trailing a sports star is that his schedule is public knowledge. You know when he'll be at the team practice facility, so just sneak in the night before and hide in the bushes until your new best friend gets there. Anyone who's not flattered by that kind of devotion isn't worth befriending anyway. Soon enough you'll be having steaks, and he'll be picking up the tab.

If fences or security guards keep this plan from working, simply follow your favorite star home. Wait until his sure-to-be-flashy sports car or SUV rolls out of the practice facility, and trail him at a distance of three to five cars. When he gets out to pick up the mail, introduce yourself. At the very least, he'll give you a handshake and the free detergent sample the postman just left.

In the event that these airtight tactics fail, it's time to take your show on the road. Professional athletes always talk about being lonely when they travel, so do your favorite player a favor and go with him. Find out which hotel the team's staying in, then endeavor to locate his room. Most stars stay under an assumed name, you say? *No problema!* Just borrow a room-service cart and uniform, and knock on doors until you find him. Then give him the real room-service entrée: friendship, with a side of devotion!

If that doesn't work, handcuff him to the radiator in his hotel room and ask him about his favorite books and movies. The cops will be there soon, but man, will you guys spend some good time together.

**When it comes to hanging out,
always go with quality over quantity.**

Geoffrey Huish

A fan of the Welsh national rugby club, Huish, 31, vowed to cut off his own testicles if his beloved team somehow managed to beat England. They did. And so he did— with a pair of blunt wire clippers. It took him 10 minutes.

Cutting off your own tackle after a *loss* might not even get you into the Top 125. But after a *win*? That's hard-core.

Index

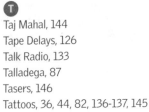

ACKNOWL

Ethan Trex

I'd like to thank Randy Moss for giving me a role model and Duke basketball for teaching me how to loathe.

Spencer Hall

Thanks to Mary Ann and to Urban Meyer—both national champions in my book.

EDGMENTS

Amir Blumenfeld

To my parents, who gave me a sports almanac on my eighth birthday ... instead of a party. Come to think of it, that's what I got every year. Thanks anyway.

Warren St. John

Thanks to Amir, Ethan, Spencer, Chris Raymond, and everyone at ESPN, Landon Webb, and Stuart Rogers, Sam Eckersley and Jane Huschka from RED. I especially acknowledge all the hardworking bookstore employees across the land, particularly those who signed the secret pact to defy their bosses by keeping this volume face-out on the shelves long past its publication date. We'll meet you under the bridge at the appointed time.

ABOUT THE AUTHORS

Amir Blumenfeld was born in Israel and moved to California at the age of 2. He felt his family needed a change of scenery, and who were they to disagree with a talking baby? Since then, Amir has moved to New York to become a full time co-author. He was one of several writers for *The CollegeHumor Guide to College and Faking It: How to Seem Like a Better Person Without Actually Improving Yourself.* Amir's work has also appeared online at CollegeHumor.com and on newsstands in *ESPN The Magazine.* No, seriously.

....

Spencer Hall is author and editor of the insanely popular college football blog EveryDayShouldBeSaturday. A Florida Gators fan, he runs a reptile petting zoo on Highway 78 outside Destin, Florida, which he never leaves. He dedicates this book to his parole officer, Sgt. Heinrich Jackboots of the Florida Department of Corrections.

....

Ethan Trex has written a weekly humor column on SportsIllustrated.com and is a co-author of *The CollegeHumor Guide to College and Faking It: How to Seem Like a Better Person Without Actually Improving Yourself.* He currently contributes jokes to *ESPN The Magazine.* NBA fans may know Trex a little better as Vernon Maxwell, an assumed name under which he played professional basketball for several seasons.

....

Warren St. John is the author of *Rammer Jammer Yellow Hammer: A Journey into the Heart of Fan Mania*, an ESPN notable book, one of *Sports Illustrated's* 10 best books of 2004, and, according to the *Chronicle of Higher Education*, the best book ever written about college sports. How he got hooked up with the guys listed above is anyone's guess.

ESPN

GUIDE TO

PSYCHO
FAN

BEHAVIOR

WWW.PSYCHOFAN.COM